Famous Women in Sports

by Kara Race-Moore

Scott Foresman
is an imprint of

Glenview, Illinois • Boston, Massachusetts • Chandler, Arizona
Upper Saddle River, New Jersey

Photographs

Every effort has been made to secure permission and provide appropriate credit for photographic material. The publisher deeply regrets any omission and pledges to correct errors called to its attention in subsequent editions.

Unless otherwise acknowledged, all photographs are the property of Pearson Education, Inc.

Photo locators denoted as follows: Top (T), Center (C), Bottom (B), Left (L), Right (R), Background (Bkgd)

Cover Keystone Pictures USA/Alamy Images; **1** Bain News Service/Prints & Photographs Division, Library of Congress; **3** Library of Congress; **4** Bain News Service/Prints & Photographs Division, Library of Congress; **6** Allsport Hulton/Archive/Getty Images; **7** Bettmann/Corbis; **8** Bettmann/Corbis; **11** Ernest C. Withers/Minnesota Historical Society/Corbis; **12** Keystone Pictures USA/Alamy Images; **14** CSU Archives/Everett Collection Inc/Alamy Images; **15** Monty Fresco/Daily Mail/Rex Features/Alamy Images; **17** CSU Archives / Everett Collection Inc/Alamy Images; **19** Associated Newspapers/Daily Mail/Rex/Alamy Images; **21** Corbis; **22** Toshifumi KITAM Agence France Presse/NewsCom.

ISBN 13: 978-0-328-52066-4
ISBN 10:　　0-328-52066-7

Copyright © by Pearson Education, Inc., or its affiliates. All rights reserved.
Printed in the United States of America. This publication is protected by copyright, and permission should be obtained from the publisher prior to any prohibited reproduction, storage in a retrieval system, or transmission in any form or by any means, electronic, mechanical, photocopying, recording, or likewise. For information regarding permissions, write to Pearson Curriculum Rights & Permissions, One Lake Street, Upper Saddle River, New Jersey 07458.

Pearson® is a trademark, in the U.S. and/or in other countries, of Pearson plc or its affiliates.

Scott Foresman® is a trademark, in the U.S. and/or in other countries, of Pearson Education, Inc., or its affiliates.

11 12 V0FL 16 15 14

Women in Sports: A Brief Overview

In the 1800s women were allowed to play very few organized sports. They could play croquet and badminton or enter archery tournaments. Most other sports were restricted to men only. And only men were allowed to compete at the first modern Olympic Games, held in 1896.

By the beginning of the 1900s, change was in the air. Women were working for the right to vote, own property, and work for the same wages as men. They were also fighting for the right to compete in sports. The 1900 Olympics showed signs of progess. At those Olympic Games, women were allowed to compete in tennis, golf, sailing, equestrian events, and croquet. Today, girls and women participate in all sports, at all levels.

In the early 1900s, golf was one of the few sports that women were allowed to play.

Trudy Ederle: The Super Swimmer

Gertrude "Trudy" Caroline Ederle was born in 1906. She was a child of German immigrants living in New York City.

Ederle learned to swim when she was very young. At the age of twelve, she swam the eight-hundred-yard freestyle in thirteen minutes and nineteen seconds. This made her the youngest person to break a world record.

Trudy held eighteen world swimming records by the time she was seventeen. She was also a member of the United States Olympic swimming team. She won a gold medal and two bronze medals at the 1924 Olympics.

Trudy Ederle

In 1925 Trudy tried to swim across the English Channel. Although she failed, she refused to admit **weakness.** On August 6, 1926, she set off again from the coast of France. She was nineteen. The water was very rough that day. Trudy would not quit and swam on despite big waves and seasickness.

It took Ederle fourteen hours and thirty-one minutes to swim the thirty-five miles that separated England from France. Her time was two hours faster than the previous record set in 1875 by a British Navy captain.

Trudy had proven that she was a great swimmer. She became an international celebrity overnight. She returned home to America as the first major sports heroine. Thousands of people lined the streets of New York City to cheer when she arrived home.

Ederle was inducted into the International Swimming Hall of Fame in 1965. She joined the International Women's Sports Hall of Fame in 1980. She was one of the first women athletes to be recognized. But she quickly was followed by others.

Babe Didrikson

Babe Didrikson: The Great Athlete

Mildred "Babe" Didrikson was born in 1914 in Port Arthur, Texas. She was given the nickname "Babe" because people thought she played baseball as well as Babe Ruth. As a child Didrikson played basketball, golf, and baseball. She also did track and field, diving, swimming, tennis, and bowling.

Babe won two gold medals for track and field in the 1932 Olympics. She would have won a third but was disqualified by the high jump judges. They disqualified her because they thought her style of diving headfirst over the bar was inappropriate!

After the Olympics, Babe became a professional golfer. She was the first American woman to win the British Women's Amateur Tournament. As a golfer Didrikson broke the standards for how a "lady" played golf. She hit long drives when women were expected to take dainty shots.

Didrikson didn't care that people were shocked by her long drives. She was determined to win. She knew that she would do better by hitting the ball as far as she could. She won fifty-five tournaments, including ten majors. Three of them were U.S. Opens.

Didrikson was never afraid to speak her mind. Then she'd show people what she could do. In 1949 she helped form the Ladies Professional Golf Association to support women's golf.

Babe spent the last three years of her life battling cancer, but she kept playing golf. She had surgery to try to remove the cancer. Afterward, she returned to the golf course and won the U.S. Women's Open in 1954. Didrikson died in 1956. She is still remembered as one of the greatest athletes ever, male or female.

Babe Didrikson changed women's golf forever with her long drives.

Women's Baseball: A League of Their Own

While Babe Didrikson was changing women's golf, other women were breaking into baseball. During World War II many major league baseball players went to war. Chicago Cubs owner Phil Wrigley set up the All-American Girls Professional Baseball League (AAGPBL) in 1943. He was worried that there weren't going to be enough men to play baseball during the war.

Dorothy Kamenshek, born in 1925, was one of the AAGPBL's best players. Kamenshek played first base. She won back-to-back batting titles in 1946 and 1947. She was an excellent hitter and rarely struck out. Dorothy could bunt the ball or smack it deep into the outfield. She could make any hit her team needed. Her team, the Rockford Peaches, won four championships during her ten-year career.

Women's baseball enjoyed great success during the 1940s.

In 1950 the Peaches lost the sixth game of the championship series. Kamenshek rallied her teammates to win the final game. She hit two singles, a triple, and a home run, driving in five runs. Dorothy had to wear a back brace because of injuries in her final season in 1951. Even so, she was able to hit for a .345 batting average while stealing sixty-three bases.

Ticket sales to women's baseball games began to decline in the early 1950s. In 1954 the AAGPBL was shut down. Still, their memory lived on. Kamenshek and the Peaches became the inspiration for the hit movie *A League of Their Own*.

Toni Stone: Good Enough to Hit Paige

Toni Stone was another baseball player who proved women could play what had been a men's only game. She also had the added obstacle of being African American. Toni was born Marcenia Lyle in St. Paul, Minnesota, in 1921. She later adopted the name Toni Stone.

Toni loved baseball. When she was ten she played in a league sponsored by a cereal company. She would practice anywhere, even in old ball parks with rickety benches and no markings on the field.

Stone became the first woman to play for a men's big-league team. Syd Pollack was the owner of the Negro American League's Indianapolis Clowns. He signed her to play second base in 1953. Pollack signed her up partly as a gimmick to attract more sales. But Stone soon proved to be one of the team's best players.

Toni had to put up with the **mocking** from other players. Teammates would tell her that she belonged in the kitchen. But Toni refused to quit the game she loved.

Toni Stone was a good enough batter to get a hit off of the legendary Satchel Paige in 1953.

In 1953 Toni had the chance to bat against the legendary pitcher Satchel Paige. It was her most memorable moment playing baseball. Paige had a **fastball** that almost no one could hit. He would ask batters how they wanted him to throw the ball—high, low, or down the middle. He would complete his **windup** and throw what the players asked for. They still couldn't hit the ball.

When Stone went to bat against Paige, she jokingly asked only that he not hurt her. Yet Toni got a hit right over second base! She was the only player to get a hit off of Paige during that game.

Stone was inducted into the International Women's Sports Hall of Fame in 1993. Three years later she died.

Althea Gibson: Pioneer in Women's Tennis

Another African American woman athlete who broke records and expectations was Althea Gibson. Althea was born in South Carolina in 1927. She grew up in New York City.

As a young girl, Gibson often played paddle tennis. She once won a tournament. Buddy Walker, a Harlem jazz musician, noticed her playing and suggested she might do well at regular tennis.

Althea learned to play at Harlem's Cosmopolitan Tennis Club. She became very good. She went on to win the American Tennis Association's women's singles tournament ten years in a row.

By 1951 Althea was at the top of her game. That year she qualified to enter the English tournament at Wimbledon. She became the first African American to play at Wimbledon.

In 1955 Gibson toured the world as a member of a national tennis team supported by the U.S. State Department. Later, she won many international events, including the French, English, and U.S. championships. In 1957 she won the doubles and singles events at Wimbledon. She returned home a national heroine. Her hometown greeted her with a ticker tape parade.

Althea Gibson was inducted into the National Lawn Tennis Hall of Fame, the International Tennis Hall of Fame, and the Black Athletes Hall of Fame.

Gibson died in 2003, knowing of the tennis victories of Serena and Venus Williams. The Williams sisters' successes are possible because of the groundbreaking work of Althea Gibson. Gibson was a **unique** athlete who broke through many barriers in women's sports.

Althea Gibson was a dominant tennis player during the 1950s.

Billie Jean King's win against Bobby Riggs was nationally televised.

Billie Jean King: A Tennis King

Billie Jean King was born in 1943. She was the daughter of a fireman and a homemaker. She grew up to become a successful professional tennis player. It angered her that men earned larger prizes for winning tennis tournaments than women did. In 1970, King and several other women tennis players were upset that the tournament judges were still not giving equal prizes. So, they established the first successful women's professional tennis tour.

In 1971 King became the first female athlete to win more than $100,000 in annual prize money. Her most famous moment as a tennis player came in 1973. That year she beat Bobby Riggs in a tennis match titled the "Battle of the Sexes." The match was nationally televised. King's win proved to the whole country that women could excel at sports too. King had been nervous before the match, but she found the **confidence** to play, and won.

Then, in 1974, King played a key role in helping to establish the Women's Sports Foundation, or WSF. The WSF works to make it possible for all girls and women to participate in sports.

Billie Jean King won thirty-nine Grand Slam titles and 695 match victories during a sports career that lasted two decades. By helping to found the WSF, King ensured that the women who followed her would have an easier time entering the sports world. Even now King still helps promote women's athletics.

Rosemary Casals: Rising to Greatness

Rosemary Casals, an Hispanic tennis player, energized the sport of tennis as she fought to prove herself on the courts.

Rosemary was born in 1948 in San Francisco, California. Her parents were immigrants from El Salvador. When Casals was only a year old, her parents felt they were unable to care for her. So she was raised by her Uncle Manuel and Aunt Maria. Manuel taught Rosemary to play tennis. He remained her coach throughout her career.

Casals felt different because she was poor. Other children arrived at the public tennis courts dressed in fancy clothes and carrying brand new rackets. Rosemary did not have these things. She was also at a disadvantage because she was shorter than almost all the other players. Casals had to prove herself through her game. And she did.

Rosemary rebelled against the traditions of tennis. She played against older girls. She rebelled against the "feeling" that tennis had at that time. She was not what the fans or the players expected.

Despite coming from a poor background, Rosemary Casals rose up to achieve tennis greatness.

Historically, tennis had been a sport for the wealthy. Players wore expensive white outfits, and the crowd would clap only rarely and very quietly.

Casals wore brightly colored outfits and expected the crowd to show more enthusiasm for her hard work. She was almost excluded from her first Wimbledon games for not wearing white. Today, bright outfits and cheering crowds are found at most tennis tournaments. This is thanks in part to the trailblazing work of Rosemary Casals.

In 1966, Casals started playing in doubles tournaments with Billie Jean King. Casals and King became one of the best doubles teams in the history of women's tennis.

Casals and King were a great match as teammates. Casals also fought for the rights of female tennis players. She worked with King to get female tennis players the same prize money that male tennis players received. Throughout her career Casals worked to better the sport of women's tennis.

Rosemary Casals created a sensation in the world of tennis with her brightly colored outfits.

After knee surgery in 1978, Casals took a break from playing tennis. Since 1981 she has been president of Sportswomen, Inc. This is a California company she formed to promote tennis tournaments for older female players. In 1990 she teamed up again with Billie Jean King to win the U.S. Open Senior women's doubles championship.

Female Marathoners: Fighting to Race

Women such as Althea Gibson, Billie Jean King, and Rosemary Casals fought for equality on the tennis courts. At the same time, women such as Roberta Gibb, Katherine Switzer, and Nina Kuscsik fought for the right to run.

In the 1960s women were not allowed to run in the Boston Marathon. Roberta Gibb decided to test this. In 1966, after putting on a hooded sweatshirt to hide her identity, she joined the race. She ran the entire race. Afterward, officials refused to acknowledge that a woman had run the Boston Marathon.

The next year Katherine Switzer decided that she wanted to run the race. On the race application she wrote her name, 'K. V. Switzer,' so officials wouldn't know she was a woman. They sent her an official number.

Four miles into the marathon, a race official realized Switzer was a woman and tried to drag her out of the race. She outran him while other runners deliberately ran in front of the official to prevent him from stopping her. Switzer finished the race.

Katherine Switzer had to fight off this race official in order to finish the 1967 Boston Marathon.

Newspaper photographers took pictures of Switzer while the marathon official tried to drag her away. Despite this event, marathon officials still refused to allow women to run. This led to a five-year legal battle. Finally, in 1972 Nina Kuscsik became the first woman to officially run in the Boston Marathon.

Meanwhile Switzer continued to work for female athletes' rights. She convinced Avon, the world's largest cosmetics corporation, to sponsor a series of women's races. Today Switzer continues to run and fight for equality.

Fu Mingxia: Diving Into Success

Fu Mingxia was born in 1978 in Wuhan, China. She started diving before she knew how to swim. To help, her coaches tied a rope around her waist so they could pull her out of the water after her dives.

Mingxia said that when she first started diving she was "scared to death." According to the rules, a diver could not climb back down the ladder once he or she had climbed up. Mingxia was always afraid, but never climbed back down the ladder.

When Mingxia was eleven she was selected for the Chinese Junior diving team. Shortly after she won a gold medal in platform diving at the 1990 Goodwill Games. Mingxia's career as a world champion diver had been launched.

Fu Mingxia conquered her fears to become an Olympic diver.

Six months later Mingxia finished first in the ten-meter platform competition at the 1991 world championships. At twelve years old she had become the youngest world champion ever. Next she won a gold medal at the 1992 Olympics. She was the youngest person to win an Olympic gold medal since 1936. She was the youngest Olympic diving champion ever.

At the 1996 Olympics, Mingxia won both the ten-meter platform and three-meter springboard diving event. Mingxia took the next few years off for school. Then, in the 2000 Olympics, Mingxia again took home gold in the three-meter springboard diving event. Training and competing brought injuries and hardship, but Mingxia always pressed on.

Over the past hundred years, female athletes have broken down many barriers. From Ederle's swimming to Mingxia's diving, they have inspired us with their feats. Thanks to their pioneering efforts, today's women can participate in and excel at whichever sports they choose!

Glossary

confidence *n.* firm belief in yourself.

fastball *n.* a pitch thrown at high speed.

mocking *v.* the act of laughing at; making fun of.

outfield *n.* the part of a baseball field beyond the diamond or infield.

unique *adj.* having no like or equal; being the only one of its kind.

weakness *n.* a weak point; slight fault.

windup *n.* a swinging movement of the arms while twisting the body just before pitching the ball.

Reader Response

1. Using a chart like the one below, write down one fact and one opinion about each woman mentioned below. The opinion should be an opinion stated in the book, and not an opinion of your own.

Player	Fact	Opinion
Babe Didrikson		
Althea Gibson		
Billie Jean King		
Rosemary Casals		

2. What questions would you have for the official who tried to drag Katherine Switzer from the marathon? How does questioning help you understand the book better?

3. *Unique* starts with the letters *uni-*. What other words do you know that start with those letters? Write sentences for two of them.

4. Choose one of this book's photographs and explain how it adds to what you have learned from the text.

Suggested levels for Guided Reading, DRA,™ Lexile,® and Reading Recovery™ are provided in the Pearson Scott Foresman Leveling Guide.

Social Studies

Genre	Comprehension Skills and Strategy	Text Features
Biography	• Fact and Opinion • Compare and Contrast • Ask Questions	• Captions • Heads • Glossary

Scott Foresman Reading Street 5.1.4

Scott Foresman is an imprint of

ISBN-13: 978-0-328-52066-4
ISBN-10: 0-328-52066-7